THE WEATHER

© 1992 Franklin Watts

First published in the United States
in 1992 by Franklin Watts, Inc.

Library of Congress Cataloging-in-Publication Data

Richardson, Joy.
    The weather/by Joy Richardson.
        p.   cm. — (Picture science)
    Includes index.
    Summary: Introduces different weather patterns in the northern
hemisphere and around the world.
    ISBN 0-531-14164-0
    1. Weather—Juvenile literature. 2. Northern Hemisphere—Climate-
-Juvenile literature.   [1. Weather.]   I. Title.   II. Series.
QC981.3.R53   1992
551.5—dc20   91-43715
                                                                   CIP AC

Editor: Sarah Ridley
Designer: Janet Watson
Illustrator: Linda Costello

Photographs: Eye Ubiquitous 7; Chris Fairclough
Colour Library 28; Robert Harding Picture Library
front cover, 10, 14, 23, 24; Hutchison Library 17, 21;
ZEFA 9, 13, 18, 27.

Printed in Singapore.

PICTURE SCIENCE

THE WEATHER

Joy Richardson

FRANKLIN WATTS
New York • London • Toronto • Sydney

Moving air

Our earth is wrapped in a blanket
of air called the atmosphere.
This is where our weather is made.

The air around us is always on the move.
It rises and falls as it
grows hotter and colder.

Air blows and swirls around the world,
carrying the weather with it.

Wind

Air on the move is called wind.
Sometimes the wind is just a soft breeze.
It rustles the leaves
and blows through your hair.

Stronger wind makes branches
bend and sway.
It whisks kites up into the air.
It fills the sails of boats
and pushes them along.

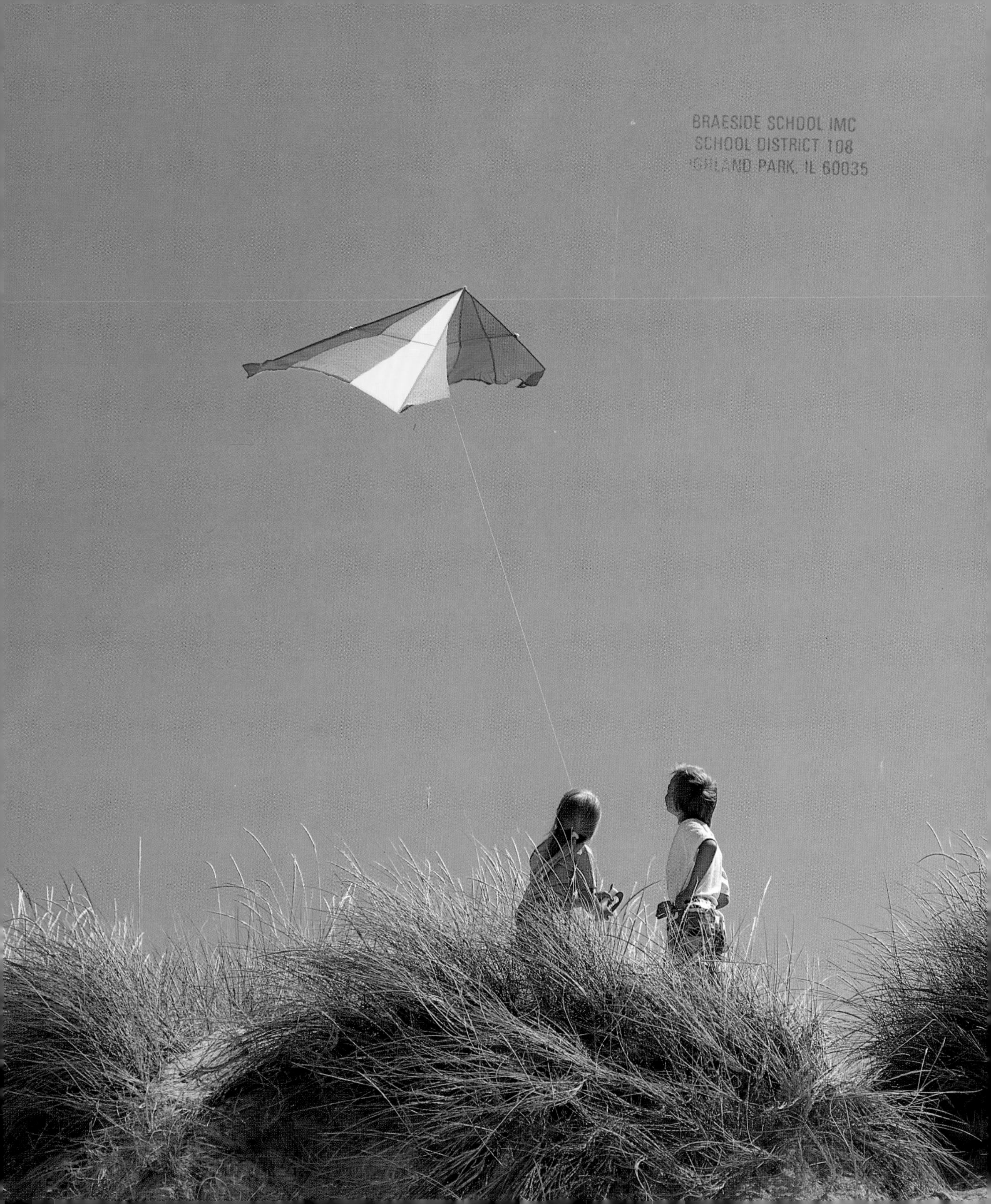

Gales and hurricanes

Very strong winds are called gales.

Gales can blow down trees
that may fall across roads.
They can make huge waves
that damage ships at sea.

Hurricanes start over warm oceans.
The air whirls around and around.
It may tear down trees and houses
if it reaches land.

Clouds

Every change in the weather
is carried by the wind.
The wind pushes clouds along.
Gray clouds are full of rain.

Puffy clouds sometimes bring showers
and then blow on their way.

If the sky is gray all over
it may rain for a long time.

When dark clouds pile up
there may be a storm.

Rain

Clouds are made of water.

Water dries up from the earth and changes into a gas called water vapor. Warm air carries it up into the sky.

As the vapor cools down, it turns into tiny water droplets which collect together in clouds.

The droplets join up and sink to the bottom of the cloud. Heavy raindrops fall out onto the ground.

Snow

If it is freezing cold in the cloud,
the water vapor turns to ice.
The ice crystals form
into six-pointed snowflakes.

Snowflakes fall out of the clouds.
If they meet warm air
they turn into rain.
If they keep cold
they fall as snow.

Snowflakes take up a lot of space.
Snow piles up quickly on the ground.

Frost and fog

On cold winter mornings,
frost lies on roads and paths
and clings to leaves and stalks.

Frost is made of water vapor
that freezes into ice crystals
on cold surfaces.

Fog is a cloud on the ground.
If the earth is cold,
it cools the warmer air above it.
The water vapor in the air
turns into droplets.
They make a misty cloud.

Sunshine

The sun shines on us all day
but we can only see it when
there are no clouds in the way.

Sunny days are not all the same.

If there is a breeze blowing,
it keeps you feeling cool.

If there is a lot of water vapor
in the air it feels hot and sticky.

Changing weather

The sun is the engine which drives all our weather.

The sun's rays heat the earth. The earth warms the air above it.

The warm air rises and cool air sinks down to take its place. This circling pattern sets off all the air movements that make our weather.

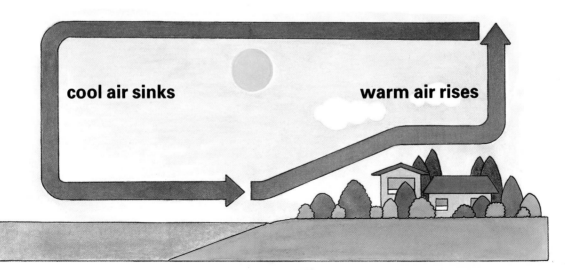

cool air sinks   warm air rises

SAT.-BILD VIS
27.9.83 09:00-09:00 Z
DEUTSCHER WETTERDIENST
0CF54

Weather forecast

Weather forecasters study
how the air is moving.

Far above the earth,
satellites take pictures
of the clouds.
Forecasters try to work out
what will happen next.
They make good guesses
but they can never be sure.

If the wind changes slightly,
the rain may pass over
and fall somewhere else.

The climate

The normal pattern of weather
is called the climate.

Our climate depends on our
position on the earth and
our distance from the sun.

The climate tells us
how hot, cold, or wet
it is likely to be
in our part of the world
at different times of year.

Weather surprises

The weather can change
from day to day, or from
one minute to the next.

The weather affects what we
wear and what we do.

People have always kept
an eye on the weather
to see what surprises
it has in store.

Index